A+ books

Alphabet Fun

Y Is for YOwl!

A Scary Alphabet

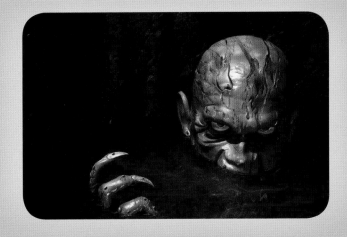

by Laura Purdie Salas

Capstone press

Mankato, Minnesota

A is for alien.

Some say aliens visit from other planets. They have big, blank eyes and long, thin fingers. Two arms? Four arms? Who knows?

2

B is for bat.

Bats hang from ceilings in caves and other dark places. You can see their small, sharp bones through their wings.

3

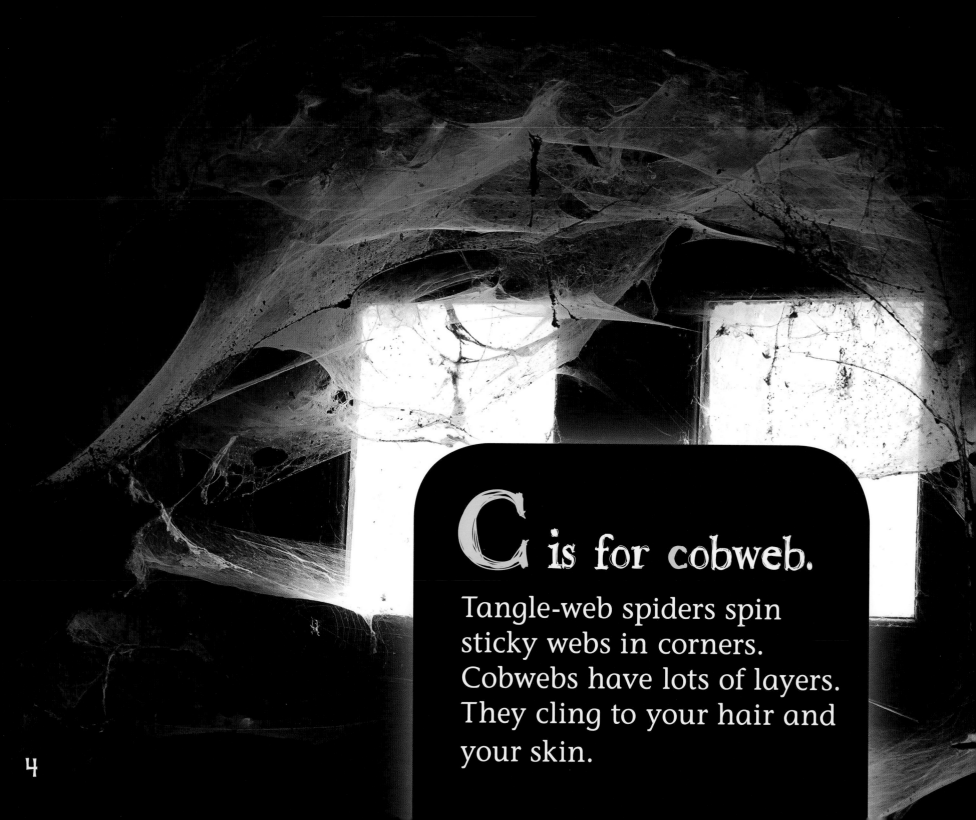

C is for cobweb.

Tangle-web spiders spin sticky webs in corners. Cobwebs have lots of layers. They cling to your hair and your skin.

D is for dungeon.

Dark, damp, and full of rats, dungeons were like private jails. Prisoners in dungeons could spend months or even years underground.

E is for eye.

It's wet and watching. Do you feel it staring at you?

F is for fog.

Fog hides secrets. You can't tell where you are in fog. And you can't see who might be sneaking up on you.

7

G is for ghost.

A misty figure lingers in an empty room. Do you see her? Some ghosts want to be seen. Others vanish in a flash.

8

H is for haunted house.

A haunted house is empty.
Or is it? Who opened that door?
Who walked by that window?
And who is moaning in the attic?

9

I is for insect.

Insects have hard, slick shells, hairy legs, and feelers. They crawl and scurry, leap and land — on you?

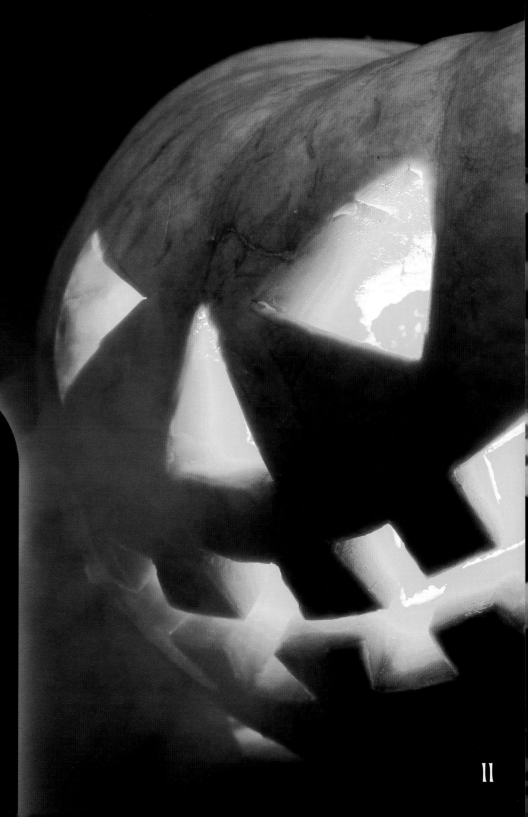

J is for jack-o'-lantern.

Flames glow bright inside a smiling jack-o'-lantern. Its face is forever frozen in a grim grin.

11

K is for knife.

A knife thrower needs perfect aim. He must hit his mark without hurting the lady. Only grown-up experts should ever try this dangerous trick.

L is for lightning.

Lightning is electricity in the sky. A bright bolt zaps the ground. Lightning can start wildfires or make the lights in your home go out.

M is for monster.

Werewolves, vampires, and swamp creatures are all monsters. A monster is not human. And most are not very friendly.

N is for nightmare.

A nightmare is a scary dream. It might include bugs, bats, monsters, and lots of terrifying things. Luckily, when you wake up, they're all gone.

O is for ogre.

Ogres are a frightening kind of giant. They are usually hairy and hungry, sometimes for people.

P is for poison.

When these fangs sink into your skin, poison called venom flows into your blood. Watch out!

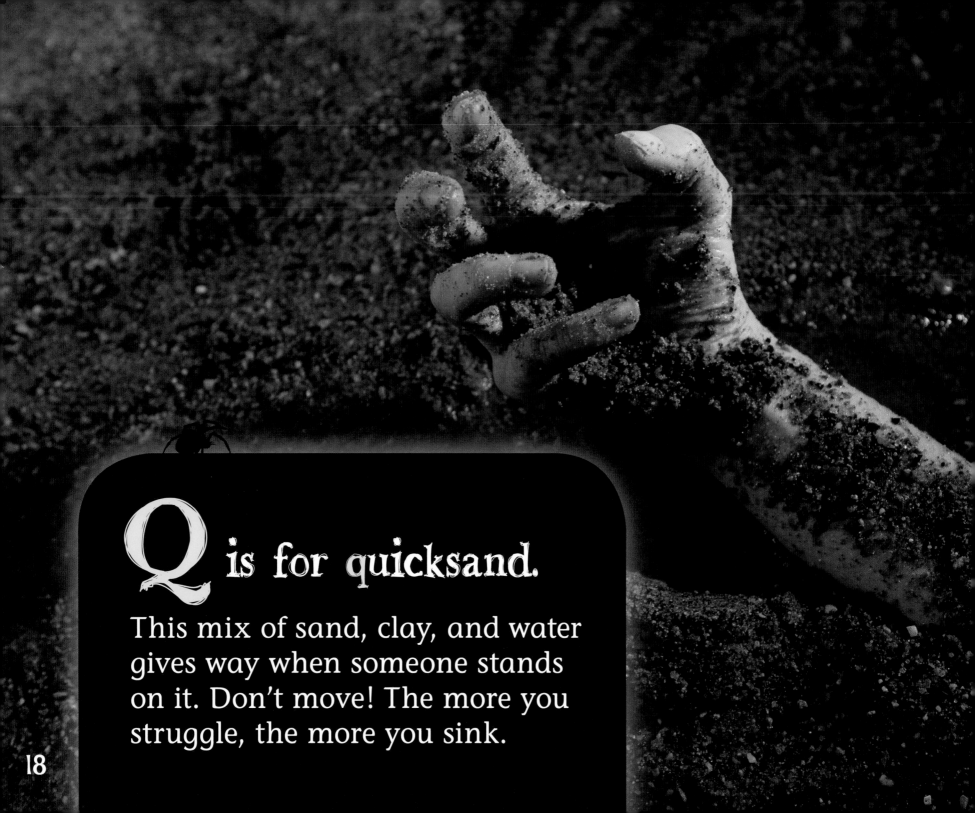

Q is for quicksand.

This mix of sand, clay, and water gives way when someone stands on it. Don't move! The more you struggle, the more you sink.

18

R is for rat.

These creatures feel right at home in the dark. They have beady eyes and sharp claws. They will gnaw on just about anything. Maybe even you!

S is for shadow.

Shadows are dark and empty. Sometimes something very ordinary makes a scary shadow. And sometimes the shadow is the ordinary part.

T is for tarantula.

These big, hairy spiders don't usually harm people. They hunt bugs and lizards instead. But would you want one crawling up your arm?

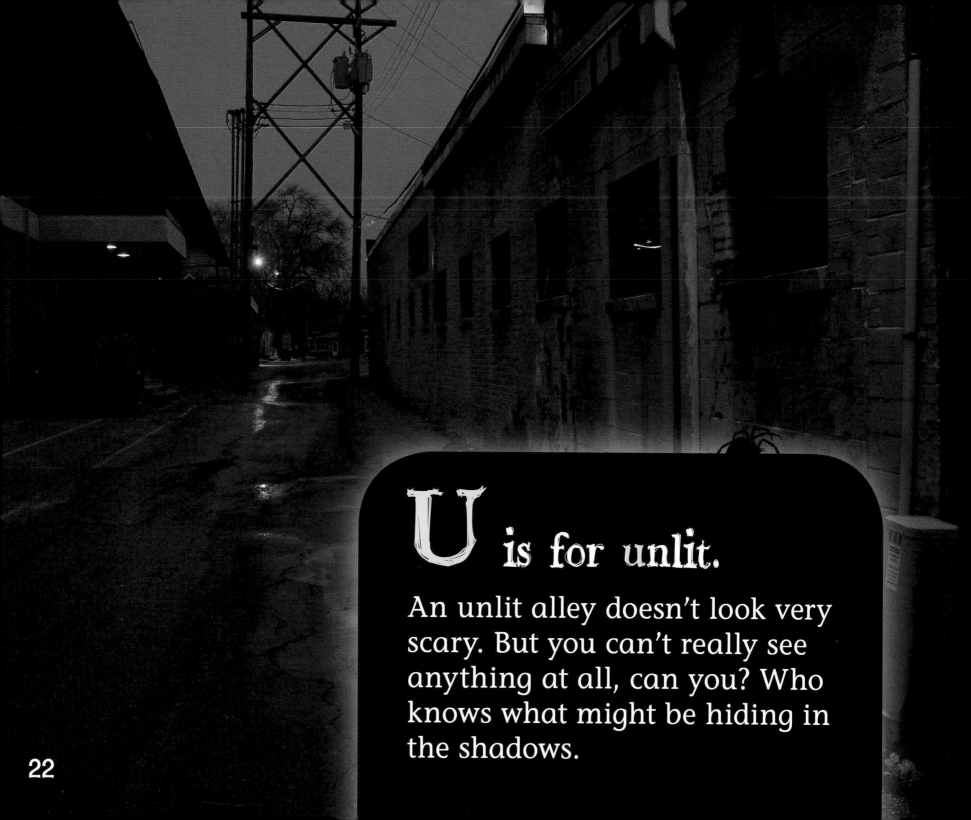

U is for unlit.

An unlit alley doesn't look very scary. But you can't really see anything at all, can you? Who knows what might be hiding in the shadows.

V is for vampire.

Vampires look like people. But they're not. These creatures love to drink blood. If one bites you, you turn into a vampire too.

W is for witch.

A witch mixes magical brew. She adds a mutt's tongue, five spider eyes, and a pinch of snake guts. Just one sip might turn you into a newt!

24

X is for explode.

Boom! A surprise explosion makes you leap out of your seat. Fireworks are scary but beautiful.

25

Y is for yowl.

A sad beast cries with a yowl. If you hear it far away, stay still. If you hear it nearby, it's probably too late to hide.

Z is for zombie.

Zombies are people who died but came back to life. They don't think or speak. All they want to do is feed. BRAINS!

Scary Fun Facts

- According to legend, the *Flying Dutchman* is a ghost ship that sails the seas forever. It can never go home. Terrible storms usually follow a sighting of the glowing, ghostly ship.

- One of the largest insects in the world is the Goliath beetle. These beetles can weigh close to 2 ounces (57 grams). That's the same as about ten U.S. quarters! It can grow to 5 inches (13 centimeters) long.

- Bigfoot is an apelike animal that has been seen many times in the forests of the United States. It stands 6 to 10 feet (2 to 3 meters) tall and walks on two legs. Most scientists don't believe Bigfoot exists.

UFO stands for "Unidentified Flying Object." All over the world, people see shapes and lights in the sky. Many people think UFOs are spaceships from other planets. But they are usually clouds or airplanes from Earth.

Some people believe that President Abraham Lincoln haunts the Lincoln Room of the White House. Eleanor and Theodore Roosevelt both said they had seen his ghost.

Jack-o'-lanterns are an old Irish tradition. The Irish sometimes carved lanterns out of turnips and other vegetables. Pumpkins weren't used until Irish settlers came to America, where pumpkins were grown.

Glossary

brew (BROO) — a drink made from soaking objects in hot water

ceiling (SEE-ling) — the top of a room

digest (dy-JEST) — to break down food so it can be used by the body

electricity (i-lek-TRISS-uh-tee) — a natural form of energy

fang (FANG) — a long, pointed tooth

grim (GRIM) — gloomy or unpleasant

linger (LING-gur) — to stay or wait around

newt (NOOT) — a small amphibian with short legs and a long tail

prisoner (PRIZ-uhn-ur) — a person who has been caught or held for wrongdoing

scurry (SKUR-ee) — to hurry or run with short, quick steps

vanish (VAN-ish) — to disappear suddenly

Read More

Clarke, Penny. *Scary Creatures of the Arctic*. Scary Creatures. New York: Franklin Watts, 2008.

DeMolay, Jack. *Bigfoot: A North American Legend*. Junior Graphic Mysteries. New York: PowerKids Press, 2007.

Fiedler, Julie. *Mambas*. Scary Snakes. New York: PowerKids Press, 2008.

Internet Sites

FactHound offers a safe, fun way to find Internet sites related to this book. All of the sites on FactHound have been researched by our staff.

Here's all you do:

Visit www.facthound.com

FactHound will fetch the best sites for you!

Index

Note to Parents, Teachers, and Librarians

Alphabet Fun books use bold art and photographs and topics with high appeal to engage young children in learning. Compelling nonfiction content educates and entertains while propelling readers toward mastery of the alphabet. These books are designed to be read aloud to a pre-reader or read independently by an early reader. The images help children understand the text and concepts discussed. Alphabet Fun books support further learning by including the following sections: Fun Facts, Glossary, Read More, Internet Sites, and Index. Early readers may need assistance using these features.

 Books published by Capstone Press are manufactured with paper containing at least 10 percent post-consumer waste.

A+ Books are published by Capstone Press.
151 Good Counsel Drive. P.O. Box 669. Mankato. Minnesota 56002.
www.capstonepress.com

Library of Congress Cataloging-in-Publication Data
Salas, Laura Purdie.
  Y is for yowl! : a scary alphabet / by Laura Purdie Salas.
    p. cm. — (A+ books. Alphabet fun)
  Includes bibliographical references and index.
  Summary: "Introduces scary things through photographs and brief text that uses one word relating to the subject for each letter of the alphabet" — Provided by publisher.
    ISBN-13: 978-1-4296-3292-8 (library binding)
    ISBN-13: 978-1-4296-3848-7 (pbk.)
    1. English language — Alphabet — Juvenile literature. 2. Alphabet books — Juvenile literature. I. Title. II. Series.
PE1155.S25 2010
421'.1 — dc22
[E]   2009011766

Photo Credits
Jenny Marks, editor; Tracy Davies, designer; Marcie Spence, media researcher

Photo Credits
Capstone Press/Karon Dubke, 15, 18, 22, 23, 24, 27
Getty Images Inc./James L. Stanfield/National Geographic, 19; Ralf Nau/Stone, 8
iStockphoto/audre, 1, 14; jacus, 4; johnaudrey, 17; LPETTE, 2; Renphoto, 5
Mark Holthusen Photography, 12
Peter Arnold/Gerard Lacz, cover, 26
Shutterstock/Andrey Armyagov, 11; Arlene Jean Gee, 7; Brian Chase, 10; Darin Echelberger, 13; Galushko Sergey, 6; Grigory Kubatyan, 3; Justin Black, 21; Max Blain, 25; Sasha Burkerd, 9; S.M., 20; Vasilly Koval, 16